ISBN 978-1-330-01397-7
PIBN 10004108

Similar Books Are Available from
www.forgottenbooks.com

HINTS ON

THE GAME OF GOLF

BY

HORACE G. HUTCHINSON

NINTH EDITION, ENLARGED

WILLIAM BLACKWOOD AND SONS
EDINBURGH AND LONDON
1895

PREFACE TO FIFTH EDITION.

THE question of "gutty" *v.* "putty" having practically settled itself, as is the manner of such, by the survival of the fittest, I have in this edition substituted for its discussion a few remarks on the merits and demerits of the "bulger"—the latest phase of golf-club evolution. This will, I hope, bring the little book, as far as its humble aims go, to the level of present requirements.

PREFACE TO THE THIRD EDITION.

SINCE the first publication of this small book. so many patients have honoured me by asking advice on so many curious forms of disease, hitherto unsuspected by the golfing faculty, that my last few months appear to have been mainly occupied in "walking the hospitals"— so to speak — in golf. I am happy in being able to say that my further experience, thus gained, fully bears out the conclusions which were at first advanced on more *à priori* grounds.

In addition to this, however, it is my pleasant duty to make grateful acknowledgment of

the numerous and useful hints I have received.
both verbally and by letter, from many noted
golfers, several of them unknown to me save by
virtue of the freemasonry existing between
golfers in all lands. Not the least valuable,
and perhaps the most frequent, suggestion, was
that I should give illustrations of the golfing
swing; whereunto my reply was wont to be,
that your golfer, combining—like the famous
Mrs Gilpin—a laudable spirit of economy with
a determination to enjoy life, would be disin-
clined to pay for his " Hints " the increased
price consequent upon such an addition. Now,
however, a further suggestion has shown me a
triumphant escape from this dilemma. As I
lay no claim to its invention, I do not hesitate
to say that the device of " demon " or " skele-
ton " golfers, as exhibited in the illustrations to
this edition, is better adapted than the most
elaborate pictorial effects to elucidate the details
of the golfing swing; and your demon golfer is
cheap, an invaluable recommendation in these

days of competition and eclipse golf-balls. To these demon figures I have appended explanations in which, and in the figures, are embodied what have seemed to me the more valuable of the suggestions of golfing friends; and thus, with all confidence and good wishes, I send forth my beneficent demons to work their will upon the golfing world.

The diagrams are placed at the end of the "Advice to Beginners."

CONTENTS.

.

INTRODUCTORY.

I READ, the other day, an advertisement of a certain outfitting firm: "The Game of Golf, complete, in a box"——comprising, presumably, several new sets of links, bunkers, &c., warranted to wear in any climate. "In a box" is good. Now if any one would only write us 'The Art of Golf, complete, in a Book'——why, what more could be left to wish for?

I am afraid no one will ever be quite bold enough to attempt that. For my own part, I have so often asserted that "you cannot learn golf from a book," that "golf cannot be played by rule of thumb," and so forth, that

it sometimes strikes me that the Fates must
have been in their most ironical mood when
they tempted me to put pen to paper to write
instructions even for the veriest novice in the
noble game. "Instructions" is too big a word.
Part of what I shall offer will be but truisms
—some truisms, however, it is hard to be re-
minded of too often—and the rest mere hints,
thrown out as suggestions and inviting contra-
diction; and even these I should scarcely have
ventured to put forward, were it not that one
sees so often men "playing golf," as they are
pleased to call it, in a style in which it is
physically, anatomically, mathematically, from
every conceivable point of view, impossible for
a human being, made on any known plan, to
strike the ball correctly.

When I first intimated my intention of writing
a book on this subject, I was immediately beset
with suggestions by kind friends of ingenious
titles for it. 'Half-hours with the Niblick,'
'Twenty Minutes in a Bunker,' and 'The Use

and Abuse of the Niblick,' were freely offered me to make what use of I pleased. I herewith gratefully record my sense of this lavish generosity; of which, nevertheless, I declined to avail myself, preferring the simple title given above.

Every scientific treatise must begin with an hypothesis; and my hypothesis is, that every man who plays golf is desirous of playing it better—is desirous of playing it as well as his natural gifts admit. It is true, and it is one of golf's greatest merits, that the poor player not improbably derives more pleasure from the game than the expert; yet none the less does the former envy the latter. Now there are many men who play badly—there is nothing surprising in that; but what is surprising is the above-noted fact that there are many men who are attempting to play golf in styles in which it is quite impossible for them ever to play otherwise than abominably. Surely it is not presumptuous to offer a few words of guidance which may possibly redeem some of these lost ones; or, if that is too much to look for, may at least keep the tyro of the future from falling into like grievous errors. The risk that the new apprentice runs of acquiring one of these impossible styles is an increasing one. In the old days there were but a few great centres where the game of golf was cultivated, and each of these was supplied with capable professional players, who, so far as might be, guided the 'prentice muscles in the way they should go. But now the game has spread, and golf clubs are being formed throughout the length and breadth of the land—from John-o'-Groat's to the Land's End. In these minor golfing centres there is often no really qualified teacher—often no good model, even, for the beginner to shape himself on. And at every golf links there is a lion in the path of every young golfer—a lion of the following nature :—

Whereas certain golfers, in each locality, in taking up the game late in life, have cheerfully and patiently topped their way through bunkers innumerable, regardless of all known rules, or, like the Cyclops of old, a law unto themselves, it has always happened that there has emerged from among the throng of these worthy men, but indifferent golfers, one who is pre-eminently unskilful. All competitors pass this unhappy wight, as he struggles in the Slough of Despond, yclept "bunker" in the golfers' tongue, and leave him behind them as a landmark amidst the difficulties whence they have emerged on to fair Elysian fields—a *pons asinorum* over which all have to pass before they can become golfers worthy of the name. With what joy, then, does not this poor lone golfer pounce upon the tyro, like a lion upon his prey, seeing in him a rival with whom he may cope on equal terms, possibly for years, probably for weeks, certainly almost for days! For the poor lone one we rejoice; but for the tyro it is a fearful thing. Nevertheless he must endure his fate. Keeping ever before his eyes the instructions of such a

Mentor as he may be fortunate enough to find, and closing them as far as possible to the distorted style of his opponent, he must struggle over this *pons asinorum* till he has proved himself thoroughly able to surmount it, and can take his place among those who, having paid their toll, look back, as we have said, with a pity which is akin to love, upon the " bridge," as on a landmark in a portion of their accomplished journey.

Then there is also a weakness which will prove a stumbling-block to the beginner even in the very teachings of those professional Mentors he will find at his disposal. It is true, golf cannot be learnt from a book ; but in the system of golfers' education empiricism has reached its limit. The tyro is told— "You must hold tight with your left hand, loose with your right ; " "You must sweep your club along the ground," &c. Now this is excellent ; but it does not commend itself to the tyro, because he does not see the reason of it. At cricket you are told to keep your left shoulder over the ball, *with a definite object*—viz., to keep the bat straight, and so present a larger surface to the ball. But at golf you are bid to do a thing quite opposed to your natural vicious instincts, which would lead you to hold with an iron grasp with right no less than left; and if you ask Mentor "Why?" he can tell you no more than that unless you follow his directions "ye canna strike the ba'." It is a convincing reason, doubtless; but it would be more satisfactory to the tyro if he could comprehend the effect on the stroke of the prescribed course of action. One does not like to feel like a parrot being taught to speak—taught to use certain muscles without the most distant notion of the result.

Now the great secret of all strokes at golf, with the exception of certain refined strokes played for the most part with the iron, is to make the club travel as long as possible in the direction in which you wish the ball to go, consistently with the application of sufficient force—that is, with sufficient speed of impact. The effect of gripping tight with the right hand is to swing the club round the left side of the body, quite out of the proposed line of flight of the ball. The proper line of motion can only be given to the club-head by grasping lightly with the right hand, keeping the right shoulder down and its muscles loose. The right shoulder down, and loose, I believe to be the prime great secret for striking the ball as it should be struck.

The professional teacher is himself but an empiric, and does not grasp the full meaning of many of the injunctions which years of experience have proved to be salutary. The beginner who chances to read this will soon, I hope, understand them better than he, and in consequence of so understanding them, will be able the more readily to assimilate and apply them. And now to proceed to details purely didactic.

ADVICE TO BEGINNERS.

I.

DO not, as is most often done, begin your first two or three attempts at striking the ball with a cleek. Begin with a short stiff wooden club—for two reasons: the mode of striking the ball is not quite the same with an iron club as with a wooden one, and with an iron club an unskilful player is more likely to cut fids of turf—*golficè*, "divots"—out of the green. This will by no means conduce to your popularity with the other players on that green. If, even with your wooden club, you should cut up turf, be careful to replace it. Golf is not agriculture.

B

II.

Begin, then, with a short wooden club. My advice as to the length of club which you should afterwards adopt, I offer with all confidence as being of a kind which the young golfer will be quite disposed to follow——viz., to suit your own fancy. Extremes should doubtless be avoided; but when we see little men with long clubs and big men with short clubs, both playing a first-class game, it is clearly useless to attempt to dictate. The same remarks may hold with regard to the weight of the heads——it is matter of opinion. Nevertheless I would here record my own opinion in favour of light clubs. More especially do I believe that the average putting of golf-players would improve were the average weight of putter-heads reduced.

III.

The ball, when you propose to play a driving shot, should be very nearly opposite your left foot, but not quite so much to the left—say three inches in rear of a line drawn from the toe of your left foot, at right angles to the line in which you hope to send the ball. It should be at such a distance from you, that when the club-head is resting on the ground behind it, the end of the shaft just reaches to your left thigh as you stand upright. Your feet should be nearly two feet apart, and the right foot slightly in rear of the left—say four inches. Such mathematical nicety may appear absurd, but instructions of " the length of a piece of string " or " the size of a lump of chalk " nature are not very satisfactory.

IV.

If, as is probably the case, you are a cricketer, I would ask you to forget all you ever learned in that department. Grasp the club with your hands close together, tightly with your left hand, loosely with your right. Some professional advisers would have the tyro keep the left thumb down upon the club—not round it, as the right thumb beyond question should be—which, however, entails a sacrifice of freedom to temporarily increased accuracy such as I should be most loath to advocate. As to the comparative merits of holding the club well home in the palm or mainly with the fingers, there is contention among the faculty. I would advise that it be held well in the palm of the left hand, and rather in the fingers of the right. Further than this I do not venture, in the face of conflicting opinions, to offer advice about the " grip "; merely re-

marking that the most easy and natural mode
is probably the best, the most strained and
eccentric the worst. In putting and in delicate iron strokes, more use is to be made of
the fingers than in strokes which require the
full swing.

V.

Remember to bring your hands well to the
front, nearly opposite the left thigh, when
" addressing yourself," as it is called, to the
ball. I venture to think this piece of advice
more important than is generally supposed.

VI.

Let your arms be free from the body, and
bent at an easy natural angle—not tucked
in to the sides in the fashion of a trussed fowl,
nor stuck out square like the fore-legs of a
Dachshund, nor, again, stiff and straight in front
of you like the arms of a man meditating a

dive into the water. The left elbow, which will naturally be more bent than the right, since the left hand being uppermost will be nearer to the shoulder, should be kept sufficiently to the front to swing clear of the body.

VII.

The preliminary " waggle," quite impossible to describe, with which golfers preface the stroke proper, is not, like the flourishes of a clerkly pen, for purposes of ornamentation merely, but is necessary for measuring the striker's distance from the ball, and for acquiring the requisite freedom and play of wrist. It is better, however, to err on the side of doing too little of this, rather than too much. Continued steadfast looking at the ball is likely to weary the eye, while exuberance of "waggle" tends either to the swinging of the club like a pendulum, or to slashing as of one practising with the broadsword—strikingly effective, doubtless, to the spectator, but not conducive to the effective striking of the ball.

VIII.

After the "waggle," let the club-head rest for a moment on the ground just behind the ball—unless in sand, when you had better not. The maker's name gives you a fine guide to the centre of the face, which is the intended point of impact.

IX.

All preliminary adjustments being thus completed, we come to the *magnum opus*—the swing proper. Now the upward part of the swing is only important for its bearing upon the downward. But in this respect its importance is very great; and I would ask you to accept this as an axiom—"that the head of the club should describe the same figure in its upward journey as you hope to make it describe in its descent." The reason of this is hard to see, but I can give you evidence of its proved correctness from the empirical side. Often, I presume, has many a golfer asked the all-wise sage: "What am I doing wrong, Tom? I'm quite off my game. What can I be doing wrong?"

"Ye're bringing up your club ower straight," will often, I daresay, have been the answer; and the advice, laid to heart and acted upon, will often maybe have set the matter right. But the matter, strictly speaking, was not, of course, that the club was coming *up*, but *down*, "ower straight." Experience shows, then, that as the club rises, so, roughly and generally speaking, will it fall, and therefore it is that I ask you to accept the axiom given above.

In this respect the upward and downward strokes are to be similar, but in the matter of pace far otherwise. I would not like to say it is impossible to raise the club too slowly, but certainly the danger is all the other way.

Golfers have gone so far as to instruct their caddies to say to them, " Slow back," so as to keep them in mind of this precept each time they addressed themselves to drive the ball. "Slow back!"—it is a valuable text to have at heart. Some write it up in their dressing-rooms, and read it every morning all the while they shave.

If then in its direction, though, I beseech you, not in its pace, the upward swing is to be modelled on the downward, it is the downward that merits first consideration.

The downward swing must, above all, be even and free from jerk—for facilitating which the keeping of the right foot slightly in rear of the left is most important. If the right foot is ever so little in advance, the swing is necessarily checked.

All the muscles must be supple; for if any of the motions in the swing are stiff, the rest are certain to be jerky. The only sinews of the entire frame which require to be tight and rigid are those of the left hand, which must have a firm grip of the club. In the swing of a first-rate slashing driver there are but two portions of his body which are comparatively steady—his head, and the toes and balls of his feet. Every other ounce of him is thrown into the stroke; and the moment the club touches the ball, the head is thrown in too.

Now as a learner you must not expect to be able to combine such freedom as this with accuracy. You must first laboriously build up your style. The head must necessarily be steady, for it is most important that you should keep your eye fixedly on the ball from the moment that the club-head is lifted from the ground until the ball is actually struck. "Keep your eye on the ball," should be your companion text to "Slow back." A golfing poet writes of

> " The apple-faced sage with
> His nostrum for all,
> ' Dinna hurry the swing, keep
> Your e'e on the ball.' "

The head *must* be steady; and just at the first I would advise the learner to keep his legs and his hips steady also—not stiff, that would be a mistake; but do not, at the first, attempt to make them take active part in the swing. Be content to swing with the upper part of the body only—and *swing quietly with that.* "Swing quietly," is a third invaluable text; or, if you prefer it in more technical language, "Take it easy," "Don't press."

The essence of the golfing stroke we have already declared to lie in making the club-head travel as long as possible, consistently with due velocity, in the direction in which we wish the ball to go. Now, if you will be good enough to take a club in your hand, you will find that this is best accomplished —always remembering that the head is to be kept steady in one position—by stretching the arms well out from the body as the club descends from above the shoulder, and then, as it nears the ground, by gradually letting them reassume the bent position into which they naturally fell when you were addressing the imaginary ball — allowing them to reach out freely once more as soon as the club-head has passed the spot where you suppose the ball to be. The club-head will, so, describe the arc not of a circle but an ellipse. Now this, though I am afraid it sounds terrifically complicated when set down in writing, is really a very easy series of motions to learn. For the first part (*i.e.*, until the club-head reaches the ball) you have a guide implied in the above-noted fact that the downward stroke is a reproduction of the upward. Tutor yourself by letting your arms gradually go to their full length as you raise the club, and of themselves they will come to repeat the motion, conversely, as it descends. For accomplishing the latter part of the stroke, after the ball is struck, successfully, two things are requisite — that your grip on the club should be light with the right hand, and that your right shoulder should work free and loose.

The club should be raised *above* the shoulder, not *round* it as is sometimes, happily not often, seen ; and if it comes natural to you to pause for a moment at the top of the swing, so much the better. The shoulders should both work loosely, but the right one more especially so. They should work as if the backbone just between the shoulder-blades was a pivot, the right shoulder being slightly lower when addressing the ball, working uppermost, of course, as the club is raised, and being allowed to swing round very much lower the moment the head of the club touches the ball. The arms must in fact be, as it were, thrown away from the body at the end of the stroke.

Do not overreach yourself by trying to swing the club too far back over the shoulder. The proper length of swing will of course depend much on your individual lissomness, but with most learners the club has gone far enough when it has reached a horizontal position behind the back. Raise it slowly, so far, and bring it down without any painfully protracted dwelling on your aim at the top of the swing.

In addressing the ball, the weight of the body should rest mainly on the left leg. As the club comes back the weight is naturally transferred to the right leg, but should again be thrown forward upon the left as soon as the club-head descends and approaches the ball. It is true, some first-rate players have acquired the habit of "driving off the right leg," as it is termed; but this is contrary to the generally approved style—on which the learner had best try to model himself.

Now these, so far as I have been able to analyse it, are the component principles of the full golfing swing, the results of which analysis we may summarise in the following didactic form :—

Bring the club, held tightly with the left

hand but lightly with the right, slowly back from the ball, gradually straightening the elbows the while until the arms are pretty well on a level with the shoulders, by which time the weight of the body will be resting naturally on the right leg. The elbows should then be bent, so as to allow the club to come well back over the shoulder, whence, by a series of similar motions in reverse order, it is to be brought swiftly, but evenly, and without forcing or tightening of the muscles, on to the ball, by which time the weight should be thrown well forward again upon the left leg, and the right shoulder be allowed to swing down in order to follow on the stroke. Meantime the head will have been kept nearly steady in one position, the eyes fixed upon the ball, until the instant of striking, when the arms should be allowed to go well away from the body, after the ball, and the head be let go to take care of itself.

After all, what have I said that has not

been perhaps better, at all events at less tedious length, said before ?——and said often ; but not a bit too often.   Keep in mind the three old texts, " Slow back," " Keep your eye on the ball," " Don't press."   Keep these in mind, and act upon them, and you will soon be a better golfer than most of us.

X.

By the time you have learned to use this straightforward swing, as I have endeavoured to explain it, tolerably correctly and consistently with all your clubs, describing shorter arcs of it for the shorter strokes, you will be passing well beyond the tyro class ; and will be discovering, moreover, that there are certain modifications of this swing, useful for certain strokes and in certain circumstances, of which the above does not give you any adequate notion at all.   These are principally two— the cutting stroke with the iron, and the jerking stroke, which is, practically, played with every club.

The object of putting cut on the ball is to make it fall nearly dead—to make the stroke as nearly as possible all carry and no run. This is most useful when a bunker or rough ground lies between the ball and the hole, so near to the latter that a ball lofted over the hazardous ground by a stroke played in the ordinary way would be certain to run far past the hole. Indeed it very seldom happens, on most links, that you are able, among the ups and downs of the ground, to pitch your ball with the approach shot in what may be called a perfectly natural way. At all events, the learning of this stroke is an addition to your power over the ball. No really first-class golfer is, so far as I am aware, without it, though some have reached high proficiency under the disadvantage of never having acquired it.

The essential principle of the ordinary golf

swing has been said to consist in making the club-head travel as long as possible in the direction in which you wish the ball to go. The principle of the cutting stroke, on the other hand, lies in bringing the head of the iron across that line. It may be applied to a full shot, half shot, quarter shot, or shortest wrist shot, but it will be quite sufficient to consider it as used in a short swing stroke —say the quarter stroke. In playing this stroke you should stand facing much more towards the line in which the ball is to go than in the full driving stroke, the ball should be more to your right hand, and your right foot in advance of the left. Again, in direct opposition to the rule for the drive, the right hand must grasp the club more tightly than the left, for it is with the right hand, practically, that the stroke must in this case be guided. Yet, mark this—though it be a principle dangerous to act on until great accuracy has been acquired—the more loosely the club is held in the hand, the deader the ball will fall. The cut, or slice, is put on the ball by stretching the arms to their full length (or as near it as the length of the stroke admits) as the club is raised, and bringing them towards and across the body as it descends again.

Now, further than this mere outline it would be useless to try to describe the cutting stroke, for the reason that you will not require to practise it till you have been learning the game some little time, will have seen it properly played, and will have made the acquaintance of capable practical instructors. Remember three points already noticed—"hold more tightly with the right hand than with the left," "stand rather facing the hole you are playing to," and "the more loosely you can hold the club, consistently with accurate striking, the deader the ball will fall." If you should find yourself temporarily "off" this stroke, you will find that you may often remedy the trouble by being careful to keep the heel of the iron well forward and down.

Remember, finally, that in iron strokes there is especial danger of the eye wandering from the ball. The late young Tom Morris, perhaps the finest golfer the world has ever seen, used to say that the reason amateurs failed in these strokes was that they unconsciously allowed their eye to follow back the shiny, attractively glittering iron as it left the ball.

XI.

The jerking stroke is a straightforward stroke, like the full drive, and unlike the cutting iron stroke; that is to say, the head of the club must, at the moment of striking, be travelling as directly as possible in the line in which you wish the ball to start—in the same vertical plane, I should say, for the essence of the stroke is that it is a *downward* one. The head of the club, in this stroke, instead of following on the ball, after striking, goes downward into the ground and usually cuts out a sod, which it is your duty to replace, or see replaced by your caddie. It is a stroke which is mostly used with the brassy, cleek or iron, when in a bad lie, or with the iron in approaching the hole. It is far easier to keep a half or quarter shot straight with a jerked stroke, for the very simple reason that since your club-head does not follow on the ball, which springs away from it while it stops itself in the ground, it is not necessary to guide the head in the direction of the ball's flight after the ball is struck. The stroke should be played with the left elbow slightly squared to the front, and the muscles of the left wrist very firm When combined, as it frequently, indeed most usually is, with putting cut upon the ball, the left elbow will need to be less to the front, and more of the work to be borne by the right hand; but by the time you are sufficiently advanced to attempt these elaborations, you will be well beyond book-learning.

With a full swing it is sometimes possible

to *jerk* a ball a long way out of a lie which it would be hopeless to attempt to negotiate with the ordinary driving stroke.   In a " cuppy " lie, for instance, it is possible to bring the club-head down just between the hinder edge of the cup and the ball, which will spring off it and fly, if accurately struck, nearly as far as from the tee.   You require to have the ball a little more to the right than in the ordinary drive— about midway between the feet—and to allow your arms and shoulders, especially the right arm and shoulder, to come very well and freely down as the ball is struck.   Remember always, that while there is a jerk as the club strikes the ball, there must be no jerking motions in the swing, and take pains in all half-swing shots to bring the club-head well and slowly away from the ball before striking.

XII.

When you have learnt all this, which no man, fortunately, has ever yet done perfectly, you will be able to reach and approach the hole in a golfer-like style. The difficulty now lies in getting into it—in the " putting." Now, in regard to the correct position, &c., for this department of the game, *quot homines tot sententiæ* is a true saying. I do not·pretend to give instruction. Confidence and a good eye are even more all-important here than in other parts of the game. I would venture, however, on a remark or two.

Some men put *at the hole;* others take as a guide a blade of grass, or something to catch the eye, just on the line between ball and hole, and very near the former, and aim to put over that. To my mind the latter is on the whole the safer method. The great difficulty in the delicate operation of putting is to hit the ball quite true, and the great secret of hitting the ball true is to keep your eye fixedly on it at the moment of striking. Draw the putter well and slowly away from the ball before striking, strike the ball quietly and without jerk, and, as in the driving stroke, make the club travel as long as possible in the direction in which you wish the ball to go. If the ball lie fairly and be truly struck, there is no fear of making a " shove," or foul stroke, through following this advice, for the ball will always start from the club faster than the club itself is travelling. If it lie " cuppy," a jerking stroke will be necessary in order to avoid striking it twice.

It is quite possible that there may be more in *attitude* in putting than is generally supposed. I once heard an experienced golfer gravely advocate the plan of getting yourself photographed in position when you were in a vein of good putting, so that if you got off your putting at any time, you could fetch out the photograph and see if you could detect any change in attitude which would account for, and enable you to rectify, the falling off. I really do think it a good plan to note down the details of your grip, stance, &c., when you are playing well, as a means of reference whereby to detect the cause of subsequent bad play.

XIII.

There is just one other stroke which needs description, and one with which you will soon become only too painfully familiar—I mean the niblick shot out of sand. In the typical niblick shot the ball lies in a heel-mark or other cup in the sand, with the face of the bunker in front. To surmount this face, you must strike rather downwards, some two or three inches behind the ball. The exact distance will depend on the height and nearness of the cliff of the bunker, and the consistency of the sand. The looser the sand, and the higher and nearer the cliff, the farther you must aim behind the ball in order to make it rise straight enough off the club. I may safely say that this is the only stroke in golf in which you ought not to keep your eye on the ball. Your eye should be fixed on the exact spot at which you wish the niblick-head to cleave the sand.

This is an unpleasant subject to linger on. You will soon have more than enough of it in practice. However, the more you know about it, the less you will have to use it.

XIV.

Remember that you do not want to hit the ball on the top, and therefore that it is not on the top of the ball that you should fix your eye —as most golfers do—but on the part of it which you wish to strike. In putting, it is especially important to bear this maxim in mind.

XV.

Now, having given you all these instructions, I would now give you another final and seeming contradictory one—not to follow them with such careful and painful minuteness as to cramp your style and swing thereby. Above everything, you must be loose and free and supple.

Genius has been defined as an infinite capacity for taking pains; and, be that how it may as a definition of universal genius, it is a most happy definition of golfing genius. " Always fish your hardest," says Francis Francis: so, too, always golf your hardest. But yet you must not cultivate this infinite carefulness to the loss of freedom. The learner who consistently misses the ball in a good free style, is a golfing infant of more promise than one who consistently hits it a certain wretched distance in a stiff and cramped style; albeit for the time being the latter will always defeat the former. Do not be so scientific as to lose all dash.

XVI.

Remember that as a beginner, even under the best of auspices, you will probably be more or less in the way of the other players on the course, and that your safety, if not your very existence as a golfer, depends very much on their forbearance. Do not therefore presume too far. The friend who introduced you to the Royal and Ancient Game may indeed evince some interest in your progress, as is but proper in your father in golf, but you really must not expect every golfer of your acquaintance to listen very attentively to your detailed account of all the incidents of your first round. If you are too prolix, you must not be surprised if some of your friends are almost tempted to hope that your first round may also be your last.

DIAGRAMS

DIAGRAMS.

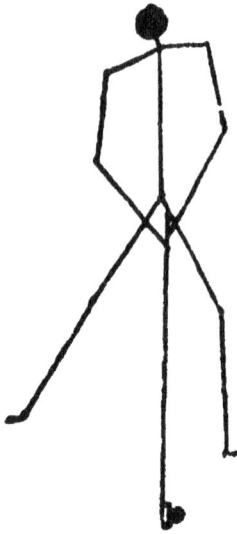

FIG. 1.—*Full drive (front view).*

FIG. 2.—*Full drive.*

FIG. 3.—*Full drive.*

FIG. 4.—*Full drive.*

NOTES DESCRIPTIVE OF DIAGRAMS.

Fig. 1 shows the position, viewed from in front, for "addressing" the ball, preparatory to playing a full driving stroke (*vide* Sections III. to VIII. of "Advice to Beginners"). The left foot must be understood to be some four inches in advance of the right (*vide* Section III.)

Figs. 2, 3, 4, and 5 show successive stages of the upward swing (Section IX.) In reverse order they are equally illustrative of the downward swing. The stretching out of the arms is emphasised in Fig. 2, in order to give effect to the written injunctions on the importance of this point as a safeguard against the tendency to "slice."

By the time the club has taken the direction indicated in Fig. 3, it will be so shifting its position in the right hand as to lie back on the web between the thumb and first finger (this is *essential* to freedom), thus further showing the necessity of a loose grip with this hand. Be careful, too, not to tighten the grip of the right hand at the top of the swing, for this is a potent and little suspected source of mischief. Moreover, though the upward swing should be slow, it should, nevertheless, be a *swing*, and not a *lift*. You should be constantly conscious of the weight of the head at the end of the club throughout the upward swing. During the upward swing of the club, the whole body, from the ball of the left foot, should wheel gradually round until, at Fig. 5, the left shoulder should point directly to the front. With a view to greater clearness and simplicity, this wheeling of the body is not fully shown in the figures, but will be amply explained by a glance at the picture (from a photograph by Mr J. E. Laidlay) on the cover of the book.

Fig. 6 is a different representation of Fig. 1, viewed from behind the proposed line of flight of the ball.

Fig. 7 shows the position for the wrist iron stroke (Section X.) In this it is to be understood that the right foot is in advance of the left. The left elbow is shown well to the front, and its muscles should be stiff. In contradistinction to the methods of the driving stroke, the right elbow, in this, scarcely leaves the side at all; and the straighter you bring up the iron from the ball (conversely, therefore, the straighter it comes down), the higher it will lift the ball. In playing this stroke off sand, it is useful to remember that shortening your grip on the club is conducive to the greater accuracy which then becomes requisite. Make it your general rule, indeed, with all clubs, to swing more quietly, to take it easier, the worse your ball is lying.

Fig. 8 is a different representation of Fig. 7, as Fig. 6 of Fig. 1.

FIG. 5.—*Full drive.*   FIG. 6.   *Full drive (side view).*

FIG. 7.—*Wrist iron shot (front view).*   FIG. 8.—*Wrist iron shot (side view).*

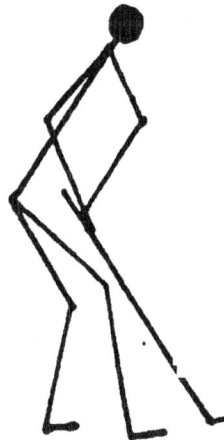

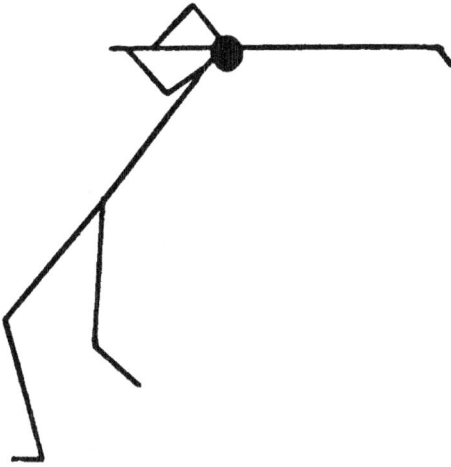

FIG. 9.— *Too rickety.*

FIG. 10.—*Too crickety.*

FIG. 11.   *Too short.*

FIG. 12.—*Too long.*

HINTS TO GOLFERS OF RIPER YEARS.

I.

IF you lose your temper vou will most likely lose the match.

II.

Most great golfers, and some others, have certain idiosyncrasies of manner and gesture, which are brought out in course of playing the game, but are quite unconnected with their actual method of striking the ball. Do not make it the object of your assiduous study to imitate these little tricks. It may be only in unessential peculiarities that your game at all resembles theirs. Genius is the gift of few, though all can affect its eccentricities.

III.

Even the worst golfer can play the game perfectly so far as observance of the rules is concerned ; yet even the best often do not. If your ball, as you are addressing it, rolls over, a quarter of an inch, from contact with your club, it is as truly a stroke as the longest shot ever driven from the tee. Do not, therefore, ask your adversary " if he wants you to count that?" or coolly replace it, remarking that " you suppose that does not matter." If an adversary makes such an appeal to you, and you have too great a regard for his feelings to insist upon your rights, you will find it a good means of rebuke, after acquiescing in *his* breach of the law, to make a similar error yourself shortly after, and when he requests you to put the ball back without penalty, to remark that "*you* always play the game." If he should omit to make this request, your case is indeed a hard one; but you need have no delicate scruples about wounding his feelings in the future. Certainly it would be far more satisfactory if it were universally understood that the game was to be played according to the strict rigour of its rules.

IV.

Do not use a long club when a short one will answer your purpose better. It is better to be five yards short of a bunker than five yards nearer the hole, in it.

V.

When lying "heavy," and undecided what club to use, bear in mind that it is better to hit the ball with the iron than to miss it with a spoon.

VI.

If your adversary is badly bunkered, there is no rule against your standing over him and counting his strokes aloud, with increasing gusto as their number mounts up; but it will be a wise precaution to arm yourself with the niblick before doing so, so as to meet him on equal terms.

VII.

Do not allow yourself to be annoyed because your opponent insists on making an elaborate study of all his puts. If you consider this "studying of the put" to be of any real assistance, you may fairly argue that his appropriating so much of the time of the match justifies you in being equally painstaking when it comes to be your turn to play. If, on the other hand, it is your opinion that these excessive pains are rather a hindrance than a help, as many think, you have still less cause for complaint.   The real sufferers are the parties playing behind you.

VIII.

Most golf grounds are public places, where the mere spectator has an equal right with you, a finished golfer.   Bear in mind, therefore, that his moving aside or his standing still, at your request, are purely acts of courtesy, and that he has a right to expect this request to be couched in terms of what is sometimes called common politeness.

IX.

Although the noted player, Mr Topsawyer, is so careful to request a person standing directly behind the line of his put to move aside, you must remember that it does not

necessarily follow from your being equally
particular that you are therefore an equally
good golf - player. Moreover, you will find
that the more you get into the habit of
making the vagaries of your surroundings an
excuse for a bad stroke, the more real and
powerful will their distracting influence become. If you can bring yourself to treat
these trifling distractions, even when they
have put you off your stroke, with the silent
contempt they merit, you will soon grow to
disregard them — whereby you will become
a better golfer, and a pleasanter.

X.

If you happen to be a really long driver, the
fact will be generally admitted without your
emphasising it, to the annoyance and even
peril of your neighbours, by always firing off
your tee shot the moment the parties in front
of you have struck their seconds. To bear

and to forbear is a necessity of golfing existence.

XI.

Do not get into the habit of pointing out the peculiarly salient blade of grass which you imagine to have been the cause of your failing to hole your put. You may sometimes find your adversary, who has successfully holed his, irritatingly short-sighted on these occasions. Moreover, the opinion of a man who has just missed his put, about the state of that particular putting - green, is usually accepted with some reserve.

XII.

Of course in every match your ultimate success will depend largely upon the terms on which you have arranged to play, before starting. The settling of these conditions is sometimes a nice matter, needing all the wisdom of the serpent in combination with the

meekness of the dove. At such times you
will perhaps be surprised to hear a person,
whom previously you had believed to some-
what overrate his game, now speaking of it
in terms of the greatest modesty. These pre-
liminaries once arranged, however, you will
find that Richard soon becomes himself again
—till next match-making begins.

XIII.

It is useful to remember, in making four-
somes, that a combination of a strong player
with a weak one will generally defeat two me-
dium players; though on paper, and with regard
to the individual abilities of each of the four,
the match may seem a very fair one.

XIV.

If you are one of the many golfers who
overrate their game, and, when constantly

beaten by those they imagine to be their inferiors, are in the habit of ascribing their ill success to indisposition, the state of the atmosphere, or even to the Government's foreign policy or the spots on the sun, you really must not be surprised at finding some ill-natured persons disposed to accept the issue of a large number of matches as a tolerably conclusive test of your powers, in preference to attributing the result to any agency in the field of politics or astronomy.

XV.

On the other hand, you should also bear in mind how, once, "the devil did grin, for his darling sin is the pride that apes humility," and that it is not altogether a wise thing to ostentatiously underrate your game. If you do so, you will be apt to raise sardonic smiles on the faces of persons whose good opinion is of more immediate consequence than that of the Prince of Darkness—whose interest is

purely reversionary.   Most men's honest estimate of their own game is quite as high as
their friends' is.

XVI.

Never, if you can possibly help it, allow
yourself to be beaten by a man from whom you
generally win.   If you do so, you are likely
to find that this one particular round, which
appears to you of such peculiarly little importance, is more talked of by your opponent than
the score or so of matches in which you have
previously defeated him.

XVII.

Do not insist on its being admitted without
dispute that the club-maker whom you honour
with your patronage is the only man in the
world who can make a decent club.   It is
quite possible that there are many golfers who
consider themselves, possibly with reason, as

competent as yourself both to select a club and to use it.

XVIII.

Some golfers, early in their career, are in the habit of giving a sovereign, or even more, for a club which they take a fancy to. The longer you play golf, the more convinced you will become that no club is worth purchasing at more than its original cost-price. Most of these fancy clubs are sold as " old Philps." Mr Philp must have been as prolific a master of his craft as some of the old masters of the painters' art. The best recipe for making an " old Philp " is a mixture of soot and varnish. On the other hand, a club which suits you, and to which you have grown accustomed, is probably worth more to you than any one else is likely to offer for it.

XIX.

Though the henchman who carries your clubs may be a most able adviser, you will seldom, as a beginner, derive much encouragement from his criticism. If he should happen to remark, " Ye learnt your game from Mr So-and-so, I'm thinking ? "——naming the celebrated player from whom as a matter of fact you did receive your first instructions——you must not conclude too hastily, and in misconception of the Scottish idiom, that this comment is an inference from what he has observed of your play. If you should unwarily reply with too great eagerness in the affirmative, the remark which has been known to follow, "Eh ! ye've verra little o' his style aboot ye," will quite suffice to show you your mistake.

XX.

Some golfers, when defeated, take a dismal pleasure in pointing out to the victor how exceedingly badly he has played, and how easily they, the actual losers, ought to have won the match.   This is a point on which you, as victor and *ipso facto* having done all that was required of you, need not trouble to enter into argument.   You may always console yourself with the reflection, that if your opponent had happened to have beaten you, he would probably have been quite satisfied with your play —though you would very likely have been less so.

XXI.

In most cases it is the loser who is so voluble in his complaints of the unconscionable time his match has been kept back by parties

E

in front. The winner is likely to regard these little annoyances with far more resignation.

XXII.

Again, if you hear a man complaining of having "lost all interest" in a match which he has lately played, you will be pretty safe in inferring that he lost it. The winner very seldom experiences this feeling.

XXIII.

If your adversary is a hole or two down, there is no serious cause for alarm in his complaining of a severely sprained wrist, or an acute pain, resembling lumbago, which checks his swing. Should he happen to win the next hole, these symptoms will in all probability become less troublesome.

XXIV.

When two golfers return home after a few days' play on a new links, it is surprising how often their opinions vary as to its merits. On inquiry you will generally find that the one who is most enthusiastic in its praise has won the great majority of matches. His must always be received as *ex parte* evidence. To arrive at a just estimate of the *terra incognita*, take into consideration the opinion of the loser also, and strike a balance.

XXV.

You will find that in most cases the winner of a match has a higher opinion of the quality of the play in that match than the loser. The latter is always willing to leave room for the inference that if he had been playing in his true form the match would have had a different issue.

XXVI.

However unlucky you may be, and however pleasant a fellow your adversary, it really is not fair to expect his grief for your undeserved misfortunes to be as poignant as your own. Remember, too, that it is not altogether impossible for him to have bad luck also, and that with such measure as you ˌmete out sympathy to him, will he be likely, in turn, to show sympathy for you. I do not remember to have met any golfer who did not consider himself on the whole a remarkably unlucky one.

XXVII.

If you find your adversary complaining to an intolerable degree of your good luck and his own bad, it is a satisfaction to bear in mind that, though you have no remedy in the present, in the future you have a very adequate one—viz., never to play with him again.

XXVIII.

Try not to forget that if your adversary should happen to get two or three holes ahead at any period of the match—even at the end— he does not thereby lose all claim to be treated as " a man and a brother."

XXIX.

Try to remember, too, that a person may be a most indifferent golfer, and yet be a good Christian gentleman, and in some respects worthy your esteem.

XXX.

You will find it pleasanter, and in the end

more polite, to be rude enough to say "No,"
should a man whom you particularly dislike
offer to play round with you. In the course
of the two hours of irritation which your weak-
minded acquiescence will ensure, it is probable
that you will be driven to say something far
ruder than the curt monosyllable which your
delicacy at first would not let you utter.

XXXI.

If you find yourself being outplayed by
the excellent iron approaches of your adversary,
it is sometimes a good plan to say to him, in
a tone of friendly interest, "Really you are
playing your iron wonderfully well to-day—
better than I ever saw you play it before.
Can you account for it in any way?" This
is likely to promote a slight nervousness when
he next takes his iron in his hand; and this
nervousness is likely, if the match is at all
a close one, to be of considerable service to

you. There is no rule to prevent your doing this; only after a time people will cease playing with you.

XXXII.

Although in general you may be a most agreeable person, you will not be choosing a good occasion for making yourself particularly so if you offer to join in and play a three-ball match with two of your friends who are just starting to play a single, without any expectation of an addition to their number.

XXXIII.

When a friend is telling you at some length of the exceptionally fine shot which he played up to the seventeenth hole, do not interrupt him in order to describe the even finer one which you yourself played to the eighteenth. The merits of your stroke, possibly even of your company, may fail to meet with their due appreciation at such a moment.

XXXIV.

When you hear a golfer enlarging upon the cruel ill-treatment which his ball suffered after " one of the finest shots that ever was played," you need not hastily conclude that the stroke was one of any really very transcendent merit. This is generally a mere golfing *façon de parler*, and should be taken to imply no more than that the stroke in question was not a noticeably bad one.

XXXV.

Remember that it is always possible to " over-golf " yourself. Two rounds a-day is enough for any man with a week or more of solid golf before him—I am speaking of eighteen-hole rounds, of course—and even then your game will probably be improved by your indulging yourself in another *dies non* besides the Sabbath. Two rounds, moreover, occupies most of the ordinary man's day, and leaves but little spare time for the lighter matters of life.

XXXVI.

To be a good partner in a foursome, you must combine with purely golf-playing qualities a certain discriminating insight into human nature. In a foursome you have not only to keep your own head and temper, but also to make it as easy as possible for your partner to keep his. Some partners require to be told they are playing very well, when they are really playing very badly. Others are scarcely strong enough for such open flattery as this. " As good as a better " is a phrase which, applied to a very bad shot, will often serve your turn in combining candour with charity and consolation. All need encouragement in one form or other.

Again, there is room for much nice tact in the giving or withholding of advice. Some play with more confidence from the knowledge that they are acting with their partner's approval. Others, a large majority, play their own game best.

XXXVII.

However badly your partner may be playing, you may assume that he is doing his best, and is far more annoyed by his bad play than you are. Advice he may possibly, though improbably, be grateful for: fault-finding can but aggravate the evil.

XXXVIII.

Most men will make a better shot with the club they happen to fancy, even though it be palpably the wrong one, than with the right one, which has been put into their hands at your suggestion.

XXXIX.

In partnership with a stronger player, it will not be needful for you to make this careful study of the times to advise and the times to refrain from advising. Ask for advice if you want it, but not otherwise. Do not think it necessary, out of deference to your partner, to be continually soliciting his opinion. It is quite sufficient to apologise once for a topped shot. Do not be constantly referring to it, as if such a mistake was a rarity. Nor when you have made what is, for you, a fair shot, apologise to your partner for "having made such a bad one." He will soon form an estimate of your game, quite apart from the effect produced by these remarks—an estimate probably more correct, and possibly lower, than your own.

XL.

You must not accept too unreservedly from a man who has just lost a foursome, all he has to say about his partner's shortcomings. These are likely to present themselves to his memory with such vividness as to throw quite into the background any of his own slight contributions to their joint defeat.

XLI.

If you happen to be much off your game in a foursome, and should observe your partner holding *sotto voce* communications with your opponents (which he treacherously withholds from you, his natural confidant), you may surmise with tolerable certainty that your own failings are furnishing him with the text. In this case your only consolation is the reflection that any show of sympathy which he may extract from such a source will be of the kind which is popularly supposed to be characteristic of the crocodile.

XLII.

Do not insult a beaten opponent by telling him, as you take his half-crown, that "he is sure to beat you next time," or that "he would have beaten you easily if he had been playing his game." He will probably reflect that if such had been your genuine opinion, it is unlikely that you would ever have started to play the match.

XLIII.

There is every reason to believe that the golf-ball is obedient to the laws of dynamics rather than to your most impassioned prayers or imprecations. Any good effect that can ensue from giving vent to the feelings must therefore be purely subjective. If profanity had an in-

fluence on the flight of the ball, the game would
be played far better than it is.

XLIV.

If your partner be one who courts needless
risks, and is about to attempt a carry which
you know to be beyond his power, you may
find it useful to call audibly for your niblick
before he has time to play the stroke.

XLV.

However hardly you may deem yourself
treated in a handicap, try to remember that
even a handicapper may be a well-intentioned
person. There is no better test of the excel-
lence of a handicap than the dissatisfaction
of all who are taking part in it.

XLVI.

That you are a very indifferent player is **no** reason that you should be placed in a position from which you are likely to win every prize for which you enter. Golf is not charity.

XLVII.

If your caddie be a lad of some intelligence, you will act wisely in letting him keep your score. No good caddie who has learnt the rules of subtraction will fail to apply them for his master's benefit. The only trouble is to induce your adversary to agree to the arrangement.

XLVIII.

If you rise to such heights of golfing powers as to attract a gallery, you will find certain penalties attaching to your greatness. Not the least, though perhaps the least often noticed of these, is the difficulty of making allowance for the influence on the ball's flight of a wind which you do not feel when in lee of the spectators.

XLIX.

The spectator has a perfect right to his opinion. It is only when he begins to act as if it were of value that you are justified in correcting his mistake.

L.

In these high latitudes you have also to sheathe yourself in *æs triplex* against the playful ways of the reporter, as · "Mr X—— led off with one of his characteristic drives—far into the whins;" "Mr Y—— laid a long put stone dead, but subsequently missed it;" and "Mr Z—— here broke his niblick—his favourite club."

LI.

If you should not have seen your partner's drive, and he should observe to you, "I think you will get a very good approach from there," you will be pretty safe in inferring that the shot was very wide of the proper direction, and that he is thus trying to account for its divergence to your satisfaction and his own.

LII.

Many golfers have a habit of observing, before playing, that they have a very bad lie, so as to discount, to themselves and others, the discredit of their prospective miss.

LIII.

When you have laid your opponent a partial stimy, it is a good plan to say to him, " You

F

cannot miss it; it is a fine guide." By thus
robbing the possible *coup* of all its glory, you
make its accomplishment still more improbable.

LIV.

When playing against a man whose pride is
in his length of driving, you will do well to
point out to him a hill beyond the range of his
practical politics, casually observing, " Young
Jehu drove a fine ball here yesterday. It just
carried that hill." If human nature may at all
be relied on, he will respond to the suggestion
by trying to hit a little harder than he can.

LV.

Driving is an Art. Iron play is a Science.
Putting is an Inspiration.

THE MISERIES OF GOLF.

I.

DISCOVERING, as you walk down to the tee to start a foursome, that your partner has never in his life played a round with a "putty" (eclipse) ball, while you yourself know that you cannot play within one half of your game with a "gutty" (gutta-percha ball).

II.

In deference to his wishes, putting down a new gutta-percha ball, and seeing the beautiful globe divided into conic sections by maltreatment with his iron in playing what, purely by courtesy, he terms his "approach" shot to the first hole.

III

On the advice of a talented golfer buying a "bulger" driver, "because you cannot go off the line with them," and finding that the new purchase invariably drives the ball quite straight —to square leg.

The question of "bulger" v. straight-faced driver is one of such frequent vexation among golfers to-day that a few remarks here cannot greatly aggravate it. The principle of the "bulger," which is a club with a convex face, rests on the very generally correct assumption that a sliced ball is usually hit on the heel of the club, a pulled ball usually on the toe. The consequence of the convexity is, that a ball that would oe a pulled ball if it were hit off a straight-faced club has the pull on it so coun-

teracted by the outward facing toe of the
"bulger" that the tendency to pull to the left
is obviated. Equally, a ball hit on the heel,
and wanting, as we may say—by reason of
the spin on it—to go to the right, does not
meekly obey the directions of the spin, because
it has contrary—left wheel—orders given it
by the inward facing heel of the "bulger." So
it drives straight—that is, approximately so.
But in order that the ball should be affected
by the shape of the face of the club, it is
primarily necessary that it should be struck
with some part of the face. And this is what
a beginner in the very early stages is very apt
not to do. He hits the ball with any part of
the club but the face, or, if on the face at all,
only on the very extreme tiptoe or the very
hind corner of the heel; and because the tiptoe of a bulging-faced club is carved away, and
the hindermost heel is likewise non-existent, it
follows that in the very early incipient stages
the chances of hitting the ball are greatly di-

minished by a bulge in the club face. What the beginner wants is a club with as much face as possible. Don't *begin* with a " bulger," then, is the practical maxim deduced from this philosophy of the " bulger." Club-makers are practical jokers: they aggravate the trouble by making all " bulgers " peculiarly short-faced. It is their little way—and they will have it. But when you have acquired a faculty of seldom missing the globe, then a " bulger " is a useful club. It drives straighter, and quite as far. If you find it difficult to raise the ball with it, get the club-maker to file the face a little spoon-wise (without taking out the bulge, as he well can). Do not be deterred by a few first wild shots all round the compass, and do not be laughed out of it by being called a Bulgerian heretic.

IV.

Describing in the club, at lunch-time, with great accuracy of detail, how, after a terrifically long but slightly erratic tee shot, you had the misfortune to lose your ball in the whins, and immediately having the same ball, with your initials stamped on it, returned to you by one of your audience, who had found it exactly in the line you indicated with such precision— but some fifty or sixty yards nearer the tee.

V.

Being asked by your opponent, just as you are starting, whether you have any objection to his wife and sister-in-law walking round with you, as he wishes to introduce them to the game.

VI.

Feeling a growing conviction, as the game proceeds, that they think very little of it—a conviction which is rendered no less painful by the knowledge that this low estimate is fully justified by the specimen of the game which you are submitting to their criticism.

VII.

Presenting one of your olive-branches, on his birthday, with a golf club, because "one cannot begin golf too young," and speedily seeing your young hopeful exhibit a gratifying promise of future proficiency in the skill and accuracy with which he drives your valuable china or your certainly no less valuable kneecap.

VIII.

Trying a few practice shots on the morning of a medal day, and breaking the club on which you consider much of your prospective success in the competition to depend.

IX.

Buying a club at a fancy price from a brother golfer, and finding that you cannot play nearly as well with it in a match as you did when trying a few practice shots before it became your property.

X.

Losing a match on Saturday afternoon by missing a very short put at the last hole, and finding the remembrance of it obtruding itself into all the religious observances and the many unoccupied moments of the Sabbath.

XI.

Just as you are deluding yourself into the idea that you are . successfully forgetting the painful incidents of a match you have recently lost, being approached by your late opponent, in a spirit of sympathetic criticism, with the remark, " I'll tell you where it was you lost that match "—which he proceeds to do; and continues doing long after the subject has, from your point of view, lost all its attractions.

XII.

Asking your partner's advice in the matter of a long approach put, and receiving from him the heroic counsel, "Whatever ye do, be up; and for Heevin's sake don't be mair than a foot beyond the hole."

XIII.

Missing a four-inch put which your partner has left you after a very fine approach shot, and receiving the cheery consolation, "Never mind, partner, never mind—another time I'll try to lay you dead."

THE END.

PRINTED BY WILLIAM BLACKWOOD AND SONS.

CPSIA information can be obtained
at www.ICGtesting.com
Printed in the USA
LVOW04s0030260416

485316LV00029B/296/P